DRAW
WITH ME

CHRISTMAS

THE TWO-PERSON
DOODLE BOOK BY:

ME & YOU

HOW TO USE THIS BOOK

Start your creative engines . . . it's time to draw together! Twenty-five delightful holiday prompts will get the two of you drawing—and talking— together! Some prompts can be done simultaneously, while others require one person to draw first and the other person to draw second. You'll also find mini conversation starters (look for this symbol: 💬) to get you talking along the way. Your first prompt awaits . . . let's go!

Published by Bushel & Peck Books, a family-run publishing house in Fresno,
California, that believes in uplifting children with the highest standards of
art, music, literature, and ideas. Find beautiful books for gifted young
minds at www.bushelandpeckbooks.com.

Type set in Providence Sans Pro, Tomarik Brush, and Six Hands.
Visuals licensed from Shutterstock.com.

Bushel & Peck Books is dedicated to fighting illiteracy all over the world.
For every book we sell, we donate one to a child in need—book for book.
To nominate a school or organization to receive free books,
please visit www.bushelandpeckbooks.com.

ISBN: 978-1-63819-219-0

First Edition

Printed in China

1 3 5 7 9 10 8 6 4 2

ME: Draw a fireplace with a log fire burning inside.

YOU: Draw stockings hanging from the mantle.
Don't forget to put names on them!

ME: Draw a Christmas tree big enough to fill both pages. That's wonderful!

Me

YOU: Take turns decorating the tree with ornaments, lights, and a spectacular tree topper.

You

What is your most cherished ornament? What does it represent?

ME: Draw the two of you in matching Christmas jammies. Just adorable!

YOU: Draw silly slippers or socks for both of you to keep your feet toasty.

ME: Draw an enormous inflatable decoration to put in front of your house. Magnificent!

YOU: Draw spotlights to showcase the new addition.

ME: Draw the snowman version of your family.

Me

YOU: Dress them up for a fancy holiday party.
Terrific!

You

💬 Do you prefer small family gatherings or large community events? What makes them special?

ME: Imagine you just came inside after playing in the snow. Draw a giant mug of hot chocolate for each of you.

Me

YOU: What would you add to the hot chocolate?
Draw an assortment of options.

You

🗨 Share
cheerful memories
while you warm up
from the cold.

ME: Draw a tray of sugar cookies in festive shapes. They look good enough to eat!

YOU: Make sure to decorate them with lots of colorful icing and sprinkles.

You

🗨 Are you getting hungry? Head to the kitchen and bake a batch of holiday cookies together.

ME: Draw a whimsical gingerbread house.
That is really creative!

Me

YOU: Who would live in your gingerbread house?
Draw them!

You

What do think it would be like to live in a house made of gingerbread? Could you resist taking a nibble?

ME: Draw a game your family plays at Christmastime.
What an excellent choice!

Me

YOU: Draw the two of you winning the game together as a team.

You

🗨 How about a friendly competition? Give each other a high five and bring out the games.

ME: Draw the ugliest Christmas sweater you can imagine. Wow, that's fabulous!

YOU: Now it's your turn. Draw everything needed to complete the outfit.

ME: Draw a pet dressed up for the holidays.
How cute!

YOU: Draw a basket of festive toys for the
pet to play with.

ME: Draw a dinner buffet with all your best-loved dishes. Everything looks so delicious!

Me

YOU: Does anyone have room left after the meal? Draw the desserts you look forward to eating all season.

You

Is there a holiday food that you have always wanted to try? How about looking up the recipe and giving it a whirl?

ME: Draw a group of musicians performing to get people into the holiday spirit.

YOU: Draw an audience enjoying the tunes.
The music is so beautiful!

You

What Christmas songs do you like most? Who's ready for a sing-along?

ME: Draw a tradition your family celebrates during Christmastime.

Me

YOU: Draw the two of you sharing this tradition with your family.

You

Why do you think your family continues this tradition? What new family tradition would you like to start?

ME: Draw the Christmas book that you would want a loved one to read to you every year. That's a great choice!

Me

YOU: Draw the two of you snuggled up reading that book together.

You

Head to your local library or bookstore and pick out new holiday books to enjoy.

ME: Christmas is a time for giving. Draw a mountain of presents collected for a toy drive.

Me

YOU: Draw a child receiving one of the gifts from the toy drive. Can you feel the joy?

You

Find a charity that accepts toys for children and donate a new or gently used toy. Encourage others to do so as well.

ME: Draw what you would like to do for people in need this holiday season. How generous!

Me

YOU: Draw the two of you volunteering together.

You

Why is it important to share our time and talents with others?

ME: *If you could have one magical Christmas wish, what would it be? Draw it!*

YOU: Draw a Christmas wish that came true for you.

You

Was your wish for yourself or someone else? What would you do with a second wish?

ME: Draw the best present you have ever received.
Very thoughtful!

Me

YOU: Draw the best present you received as a child.

You

Why were these gifts so memorable for each of you?

ME: Santa's elves work hard every year and deserve to have a bit of fun. Draw them having a friendly snowball fight.

YOU: Santa can't resist joining in. Draw him aiming at an unsuspecting elf. Watch out!

ME: Draw yourself riding on the Polar Express train to the North Pole. How exciting!

YOU: Draw one of the extraordinary contraptions in Santa's Workshop.

You

ME: Draw Santa a brand-new ride. Is it still reindeer-powered?

Me

YOU: Draw a modern Santa suit. What upgrades would it have?

You

How do you think Santa and his reindeer would feel about all these changes?

ME: Draw a plate of goodies for Santa to sample on Christmas Eve. Did you remember a glass of milk?

Me

YOU: Draw some tasty treats for Santa's reindeer to eat, too.

You

Have you ever tried staying awake to catch Santa delivering presents? What would you do if Santa caught you peeking?

ME: Draw your favorite thing about Christmas.

Me

YOU: Draw your favorite thing about Christmas, too.

You

Was it difficult to
choose? Why does it
mean so much to you?

ME: Draw a Christmas card for the person who's drawing with you.

Me ⟩

YOU: Your turn! Draw a Christmas card for the person who's drawing with you.

You

● Say "Merry Christmas! I love you" to each other. Doesn't that feel good?

ABOUT THE AUTHOR

Victoria is a doodle enthusiast who finds joy in wielding scented markers, sprinkling rainbow glitter, and creating memories with her children. She believes the best way to celebrate the holidays is to combine creative activities with family time.

ABOUT BUSHEL & PECK BOOKS

Bushel & Peck Books is a children's publishing house with a special mission. Through our Book-for-Book Promise™, we donate one book to kids in need for every book we sell. Our beautiful books are given to kids through schools, libraries, local neighborhoods, shelters, nonprofits, and also to many selfless organizations that are working hard to make a difference. So thank you for purchasing this book! Because of you, another book will make its way into the hands of a child who needs it most.